# Sower

## Stories of Faith, Hope and Love

by
*Brian Cavanaugh, T.O.R.*
*Edited by Maria L. Maggi*

PAULIST PRESS
New York / Mahwah, N.J.

*Cover design by Tim McKeen. Cover photo by Don Kimball.*

Library of Congress Cataloging-in-Publication Data

Sower's seeds of virtue : stories of faith, hope, and love / [compiled] by Brian Cavanaugh : edited by Maria L. Maggi.
    p.  cm.
    Includes bibliographical references.
    ISBN: 0-8091-3722-4 (alk. paper)
    1. Homiletical illustrations. I. Cavanaugh, Brian, 1947–
II. Maggi, Maria L.
BV4225.2.S59  1997
242—dc21
                                       96–6812
                                         CIP

Published by Paulist Press
997 Macarthur Boulevard
Mahwah, New Jersey 07430

Printed and bound in the
United States of America

# CONTENTS

Introduction ................................................................. 1

## STORIES OF FAITH

*Faith, Fact, and Feeling* .................................................. 5
*On Being a Saint* .......................................................... 6
*The Ten Commandments* ................................................ 9
*The Great Stone Face* ................................................... 10
*Become What You Want To Be* ....................................... 12
*Believe It, Achieve It* .................................................... 15
*Prince with a Crooked Back* .......................................... 16
*Who Really Loves God?* ................................................ 18
*The Gospel According to You* ........................................ 19
*Alphabet Prayer* ......................................................... 20
*The Beatitudes: The Lesson* .......................................... 21
*The Origins of the Christmas Crib* ................................. 23
*Telling One's Own Story* ............................................... 25
*On a Journey* .............................................................. 26
*God Is Within You* ...................................................... 27

# STORIES OF HOPE

Let the Music Out.................................................... 31
A Leader's Impact .................................................. 36
The Little Guy with a Big Dream .............................. 39
"Nothing Will Grow There!"..................................... 43
Work with Flaws .................................................... 45
We've Lost Sight of Christmas ................................. 47
Still Rope, Still Hope .............................................. 50
Be a Lamplighter ................................................... 51
A Ripple of Hope ................................................... 53
Answer to Prayer .................................................. 55
Growing Older ...................................................... 56
Your Easter .......................................................... 57
New Creatures in Christ.......................................... 59
Consider the Walnut .............................................. 60
Power To Fly ......................................................... 61

# STORIES OF LOVE

Grains of Caring..................................................... 65
God Searches for Us .............................................. 66
God's Pattern in Our Lives ...................................... 68
The Gift of the Magi (adapted) ................................ 71
A Mother's Paraphrase of 1 Corinthians 13................ 73

*God Who Enables*......................................................... 76
*Meaning of Christmas* ................................................. 77
*The Most Valuable Treasure* ....................................... 79
*The Wedding Ring* ...................................................... 80
*Love for Others: A Hasidic Story* ............................... 81
*On Compassion* .......................................................... 82
*Three Questions* .......................................................... 83
*Heroes* ........................................................................ 84
*Loving Your Enemies* .................................................. 86
*Reach Out or Pass By* .................................................. 89

Suggestions for Further Reading ............................. 90

# INTRODUCTION

*T*he parable of the sower found in the gospels of Matthew, Mark and Luke is meant for all of us. It beckons us to respond to the word of God—the seed planted—and to produce in the rich soil of our lives abundant fruit.

The stories of virtue in this small volume encourage us to cultivate faith, hope and love in the everyday path our lives take: at home, at work, in the classroom, amidst solitude, with companions and with God. Embrace the meanings and the messages with an open spirit—and may you yield thirty, sixty, even one hundredfold!

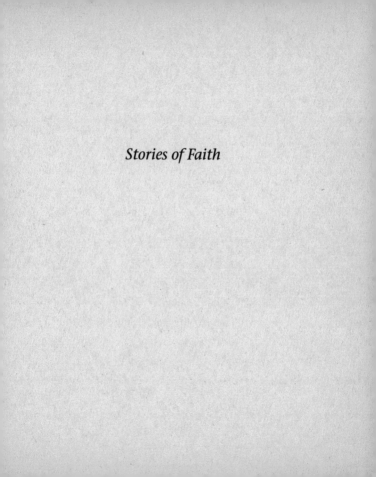

*Stories of Faith*

## FACT, FAITH, AND FEELING
### *Anonymous*

*T*hree companions—Mr. Fact, Mr. Faith, and Mr. Feeling—were walking along, one in front of the other, on top of a wall. Suddenly Mr. Feeling, who was last in line, and who was not noted for his good balance, stumbled and fell from the wall. He lay groaning on the ground. Mr. Faith, distracted by the loss of his companion, also slipped and fell from the wall. Only Mr. Fact remained. He was not moved easily, and stood firm as a rock. By doing so, he was able to help Mr. Faith to get back up. At last, between Mr. Fact and Mr. Faith, they were able to restore a shaken Mr. Feeling back up on the wall and to continue their journey.

## ON BEING A SAINT
*Anonymous*

Once upon a time, more than seventeen hundred years ago, a young man decided to become a saint. He left his home, family and possessions. He said goodbye to relatives and friends, sold all he owned, gave the money to the poor, and walked off into the desert to find God.

He walked through the desert sands until he found a dark cave. "Here," he thought, "I will be alone with God. Here nothing can distract me from God." He prayed day and night in the dark cave. But God sent him great temptations. He imagined all the good things of life and wanted them desperately. However, he was determined to give up everything in order to have God alone. After many months the temptations stopped. St. Anthony of Egypt was at peace, having nothing but God.

But then, according to legend, God said, "Leave your cave for a few days and go off to a distant town. Look for the town shoemaker. Knock on his door and stay with him for a while."

The holy hermit was puzzled by God's command, but left the next morning. He walked all day across the desert sands. By nightfall he came to the village, found the home of the shoemaker and knocked on the door. A smiling man opened it.

"Are you the town shoemaker?" the hermit asked.

"Yes, I am," the shoemaker answered. He noticed how tired and hungry the hermit looked. "Come in," he said. "You need something to eat and a place to rest." The shoemaker called his wife. They prepared a fine meal for the hermit and gave him a good bed to sleep on.

The hermit stayed with the shoemaker and his family for three days. The hermit asked many questions about their lives. But he didn't tell them much about himself even though the couple were very curious about his life in the desert. They talked a lot and became good friends.

Then the hermit said goodbye to the shoemaker and his wife. He walked back to his cave wondering why God had sent him to visit the shoemaker.

"What was the shoemaker like?" God asked the hermit when he settled down again in his dark cave.

"He is a simple man," the hermit began. "He has a wife who is going to have a baby. They seem to love each other very much. He has a small shop where he makes shoes. He works hard. They have a simple house. They give money and food to those who have less than they have. He and his wife believe very strongly in you and pray at least once a day. They have many friends. And the shoemaker enjoys telling jokes."

God listened carefully. "You are a great saint, Anthony," God said, "and the shoemaker and his wife are great saints, too."

# THE TEN COMMANDMENTS
*Anonymous*

"Before I die I mean to make a pilgrimage to the Holy Land," a nineteenth century industrial baron once said to Mark Twain. "I will climb to the top of Mount Sinai and read the ten commandments aloud."

"Why don't you stay home and keep them?" replied Twain.

# THE GREAT STONE FACE
### Nathaniel Hawthorne

In a pleasant, sunny valley, surrounded by lofty mountains, lived a boy named Ernest. On the side of one of the mountains, in bold relief, nature had carved the features of a gigantic face.

From the steps of his cottage, the boy used to gaze intently upon the stone face, for his mother had told him that some day a man would come to the valley who would look just like the Great Stone Face. His coming would bring joy and happiness to the entire community.

"Mother," said the boy, "I wish that it could speak, for it looks so kind that its voice must be pleasant. If I were to see a man with such a face, I should love him dearly." So, Ernest continued to gaze at the Great Stone Face for hours at a time.

Several times the rumor spread that the long-looked-for benefactor was coming, but each time when the man arrived, the rumor proved to be false. In the meantime, Ernest had grown into manhood, doing good wherever he could. The people in the village loved him. Everyone was his friend. And as he became an old man, Ernest was still looking for the arrival of the long-expected one.

One day a poet came into the valley. He had heard the prophecy about the Great Stone Face, and at evening, when the sun was setting, he saw Ernest talking to some people. As the last rays of light flooded the massive outlines on the distant mountainside, they fell on Ernest's face. The poet cried aloud, "Behold! Behold! Ernest himself is the likeness of the Great Stone Face."

Then all the people looked, and sure enough, they saw that what the poet said was true. By looking daily at the Great Stone Face, Ernest had become like it.

If we gaze intently on Jesus as our Teacher and Example, we will become more like Him.

# BECOME WHAT YOU WANT TO BE
*Anonymous*

Let me tell you about a little girl who was born into a very poor family in a shack in the backwoods of Tennessee. She was the 20th of 22 children, prematurely born and frail. Her survival was doubtful. When she was four years old she had double pneumonia and scarlet fever—a deadly combination that left her with a paralyzed and useless left leg. She had to wear an iron leg brace. Yet she was fortunate in having a mother who encouraged her.

Well, this mother told her little girl, who was very bright, that despite the brace and leg, she could do whatever she wanted to do with her life. She told her that all she needed to do was to have faith, persistence, courage and an indomitable spirit.

So at nine years of age, the little girl removed the leg brace, and she took the step the doctors told her she would never take normally. In four years, she developed a rhythmic stride, which was a medical wonder. Then this girl got the notion, the incredible notion, that she would like to be the world's greatest woman runner. Now, what could she mean—be a runner with a leg like that?

At age 13, she entered a race. She came in last—way, way last. She entered every race in high school, and in every race she came in last. Everyone begged her to quit! However, one day, she came in next to last. And then there came a day when she won a race. From then on, Wilma Rudolph won every race that she entered.

Wilma went to Tennessee State University, where she met a coach named Ed Temple. Coach Temple saw the indomitable spirit of the girl, that she was a believer and that she had great natural talent. He trained her so well that she went to the Olympic Games.

There she was pitted against the greatest woman runner of the day, a German girl named Jutta Heine. Nobody had ever beaten Jutta. But in the 100-meter dash, Wilma Rudolph won. She beat Jutta again in the 200-meters. Now Wilma had two Olympic gold medals.

Finally came the 400-meter relay. It would be Wilma against Jutta once again. The first two runners on Wilma's team made perfect handoffs with the baton. But when the third runner handed the baton to Wilma, she was so excited she dropped it, and

Wilma saw Jutta taking off down the track. It was impossible that anybody could catch this fleet and nimble girl. But Wilma did just that! Wilma Rudolph had earned three Olympic gold medals.

## BELIEVE IT, ACHIEVE IT
*Mark Link, S.J.*

In the "Star Wars" movie, *The Empire Strikes Back,* Luke Skywalker flies his X-wing ship to a swamp planet on a personal quest. There he seeks out a Jedi master named Yoda to teach him the ways of becoming a Jedi warrior. Luke wants to free the galaxy from the oppression of the evil tyrant, Darth Vader.

Yoda reluctantly agrees to help Luke and begins by teaching him how to lift rocks with his mental powers.

Then, one day, Yoda tells Luke to lift his ship out from the swamp where it sank after a crash landing. Luke complains that lifting rocks is one thing, but lifting a star-fighter is quite another matter. Yoda insists. Luke manages a valiant effort but fails in his attempt.

Yoda then focuses his mind, and lifts out the ship with ease. Luke, dismayed, exclaims, "I don't believe it!"

"That's why you couldn't lift it," Yoda replied. "You didn't believe you could."

## PRINCE WITH A CROOKED BACK
*Anonymous*

There once was a handsome prince who had a crooked back. This defect kept him from attaining his full potential as the kind of prince he dreamt to be. One day the king had the best sculptor in the land carve a statue of the prince. It portrayed him, however, not with a crooked back but with a straight back. The king placed the statue in the prince's private garden. And whenever the prince gazed at it, his heart would quicken.

Months passed, and people began to say, "Do you notice, the prince's back doesn't seem as crooked as it was."

When the prince overheard this remark, he gained more confidence in himself. Now he began to spend hours studying the statue and meditating on his personal dream. Then one day a remarkable thing happened. The prince reached high overhead, stretching himself. Suddenly, he was standing straight and tall, just like the statue.

You, too, were born to royalty, to be a prince or a princess. But is there a defect keeping you from attaining your full potential as the kind of person you dream to be?

## WHO REALLY LOVES GOD?
*Anonymous*

An angel was walking down the street of a nearby town. In the angel's right hand was a torch and in the left was a bucket of water. "What are you going to do with that fire and water?" a passerby inquired.

The angel replied, "With the torch, I'm going to burn down the mansions of heaven, and with the bucket of water, I'm going to put out the fires of hell. Then we'll see who really loves God."

## THE GOSPEL ACCORDING TO YOU
### *Anonymous*

The gospels of Matthew, Mark, Luke and John
Are read by more than a few,
But the one that is most read and commented on
Is the gospel according to you.
You are writing a gospel, a chapter each day
By the things that you do and the words that you say.
People read what you write, whether faithless or true.
Say, what is the gospel according to you?
Do others read His truth and His love in your life?
Or has yours been too full of malice and strife?
Does your life speak of evil, or does it ring true?
Say, what is the gospel according to you?

## ALPHABET PRAYER
*Anonymous*

One night while babysitting, a grandfather passed his granddaughter's room and overheard her repeating the alphabet in an oddly reverent fashion. "What on earth are you up to?" he asked.

"I'm saying my prayers," explained the little girl. "But I can't think of exactly the right words tonight, so I'm just saying all the letters. God will put them together for me, because he knows what I'm thinking."

## THE BEATITUDES: THE LESSON
*Anonymous*

Jesus took his disciples up the mountain, gathered them around him and began to teach them saying:

"Blessed are the poor in spirit for theirs is the kingdom of heaven.
Blessed are the meek.
Blessed are they who mourn.
Blessed are the merciful.
Blessed are they who thirst for justice.
Blessed are you when persecuted.
Blessed are you when you suffer.
Be glad and rejoice for your reward will be great in heaven..."

Simon Peter spoke up and said, "Do we have to write this stuff down?" Andrew asked, "Are we supposed to remember this?" James piped in, "Will we be tested on this?" Philip asked, "What if we don't understand it?" Bartholomew inquired, "Is this an assignment to turn in?" John said, "The other disciples didn't have to learn all this." Matthew said, "When do we get off this mountain?" And Judas questioned, "What does this have to do with real life anyway?"

Then one of the Pharisees present asked to see Jesus' lesson plans. Another demanded to know Jesus' terminal objectives in the cognitive domain...

And Jesus wept!

# THE ORIGINS OF THE CHRISTMAS CRIB
*From the Life of St. Francis* (Legenda Maior)
*by*
*St. Bonaventure*

It happened in the third year before his death that St. Francis decided, in order to arouse devotion, to celebrate at Greccio with the greatest possible solemnity the memory of the birth of the Child Jesus. So that this would not be considered a type of novelty, he petitioned for and obtained permission from the Supreme Pontiff. He had a crib prepared, hay carried in and an ox and an ass led to the place. The friars are summoned, the people come, the forest resounds with their voices and that venerable night is rendered brilliant and solemn by a multitude of bright lights and by resonant and harmonious hymns of praise. The man of God stands before the crib, filled with affection, bathed in tears and overflowing with joy. A solemn Mass is celebrated over the crib, with Francis as deacon chanting the holy Gospel. Then he preaches to the people standing about concerning the birth of the poor King, whom, when he wished to name him, he called in his tender love, the Child of Bethlehem.

A certain virtuous and truthful knight, Sir John of Greccio, who had abandoned worldly military activity

out of love of Christ and had become an intimate
friend of the man of God, claimed that he saw a beautiful little boy asleep in the crib and that the blessed
father Francis embraced it in both of his arms and
seemed to wake it from sleep.

Not only does the holiness of the witness
make credible
this vision of the devout knight,
but also the truth it expresses
proves its validity
and the subsequent miracles confirm it.
For Francis' example
when considered by the world
is capable of arousing
the hearts of those who are sluggish
in the faith of Christ.

The hay from the crib
was kept by the people
and miraculously cured sick animals
and drove away different kinds of pestilence.
Thus God glorified his servant in every way
and demonstrated the efficacy
of his holy prayer
by the evident signs
of wonderful miracles.

## TELLING ONE'S OWN STORY
### *Anonymous*

When the great Rabbi Israel Baal Shem-Tov saw misfortune threatening the Jews, it was his custom to go into a certain part of the forest to meditate. There he would light a fire, say a prayer, and a miracle would be accomplished and the misfortune averted.

Later, when his disciple, the celebrated Magid of Mezritch, had occasion, for the same reason, to say the prayer, he would go to the same place in the forest and say: "Master of the Universe, listen! I do not know how to light the fire, but I am still able to say the prayer." And, again, a miracle would be accomplished.

Still later, Rabbi Moshe-Leib of Sasov, in order to save his people once more, would go into the forest and say: "I do not know how to light the fire, I do not know the prayer, but I know the place, and this must be sufficient." Once again, a miracle.

Then it fell to Rabbi Israel of Rizhyn to overcome misfortune. Sitting in his armchair, his head in his hands, he spoke to God: "I am unable to light the fire and I do not know the prayer; I cannot even find the place in the forest. All I can do is to tell the story, and this must be sufficient." And it was sufficient.

## ON A JOURNEY
### *Anonymous*

You have been sent on a journey. You had no choice about when or where it started. You don't know when, where or how it will end. You have no map. All you know for sure is that it's bound to end sometime.

There are rules that apply to this journey, but you've had to learn them as you go. And you cannot control them. You may not even know the purpose of the journey, even though others claim to know.

All you know is that once started, you must continue every day, whether you feel like it or not. You start with no possessions, and when you finish you must turn in all you have accumulated. In the end, say some, you will be rewarded or punished. But how do they know for sure?

That's life, my friends, and you cannot change it. A little faith and a sense of humor, fortunately, help cushion some of the bumps.

# GOD IS WITHIN YOU
### Anonymous

A little girl was standing with her grandfather by an old-fashioned open well. They had just lowered a bucket and had drawn some water to drink.

"Grandfather," asked the little girl, "where does God live?"

The old man picked up his little granddaughter and held her over the open well. "Look down into the well," he said, "and tell me what you see."

"I see a reflection of myself," said the little girl.

"And that's where God lives," said the grandfather. "He lives in you."

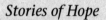

*Stories of Hope*

# LET THE MUSIC OUT
*Anonymous*

*T*hree neighborhood boys, Salvator, Julio and Antonio, lived and played in Cremona, Italy, around the mid-1600s. Salvator had a beautiful tenor voice and Julio played the violin in accompaniment as they strolled the piazzas. Antonio also liked music and would have loved to sing along, but his voice squeaked like a creaky door hinge. All the children made fun of him whenever he tried to sing. Yet Antonio was not without talent. His most prized possession was the pocketknife his grandfather had given him. He was always whittling away on some piece of wood. In fact, Antonio made some very nice things with his whittling.

As the time for the annual festival approached, the houses and streets gradually became festooned with beautiful decorations for spring. Dressed in their finest clothes, people filled the streets. On festival day, Salvator and Julio planned to go to the cathedral where they would play and sing in the crowded plaza.

"Would you like to come with us?" they called to Antonio, who sat on his stoop whittling on a piece of

31

wood. "Who cares if you can't sing? We'd like to have you come with us anyway."

"Sure, I'd like to come along," Antonio replied. "The festival is so much fun."

The three boys went off to the cathedral. As they walked along, Antonio kept thinking about their remark about his not being able to sing. It made him cry in his heart, because he loved music as much as they did, even if his voice did squeak a little.

When they arrived at the plaza, Julio began to play the violin while Salvator sang with his melodious voice. People stopped to listen, and most of them left a coin or two for the shabbily dressed boys. An elderly man stepped out from the crowd. He complimented them and placed a shiny coin into Salvator's hand. He was quickly lost in the milling crowd.

Salvator opened his hand and gasped, "Look! It's a gold coin." He clenched it between his teeth to make sure. All three boys were excited and passed the coin back and forth, examining it. They all agreed that it was a real gold piece.

"But he can well afford it," said Julio. "You know, he's the great Amati."

Antonio asked sheepishly, "And who is Amati? Why is he so great?"

Both boys laughed as they said, "You've never heard of Amati?"

"Of course he hasn't," said Julio. "He knows nothing about music makers. He has a squeaky voice and is just a whittler of wood." Julio went on, "For your information, Antonio, Amati happens to be a great violin maker, probably the best in all of Italy or even the entire world, and he even lives here in our city."

As Antonio walked home that evening, his heart was very heavy. It seemed that he had been laughed at too often for his squeaky voice and his whittling. So, very early the next morning, Antonio left his home, carrying his precious whittling knife. His pockets were stuffed with some of the things he had made—a pretty bird, a flute, several statues and a small boat. He was determined to find the home of the great Amati.

Eventually, Antonio found the house and gently knocked on the front door. When a servant opened it, the great master heard Antonio's squeaky voice and came to see what he wanted so early in the morning.

"I brought these for you to see, sir," replied Antonio, as he emptied his pockets of the assortment of items that he had carved. "I hope you will look at these and tell me if I have enough talent to learn how to make violins, too."

Amati carefully picked up and examined each piece, and invited Antonio into his house. "What is your name?" he asked.

"Antonio, sir," he squeaked.

"And why do you want to make violins?" inquired Amati, now quite serious.

Impulsively Antonio blurted, "Because I love music, but I cannot sing with a voice that sounds like a squeaky door hinge. You heard how good my friends are yesterday in front of the cathedral. I, too, want to make music come alive."

Leaning forward and looking Antonio in the eyes, Amati said, "The thing that matters most is the song in the heart. There are many ways of making music— some people play the violin, others sing, still others paint wonderful pictures. Each helps to add to the splendor of the world. You are a whittler, but your song shall be as noble as any."

These words made Antonio very happy, and he

34

never forgot this message of hope. In a very short while, Antonio became a student of the great artist. Very early, every morning, he went to Amati's workshop, where he listened and learned and watched his teacher. After many years, there was not one secret about the making of a violin, with all of its seventy different parts, that he did not know. By the time he was twenty-two years old, his master allowed him to put his own name on a violin he had made.

For the rest of life, Antonio Stradivari made violins—more than 1,100 of them—trying to make each one better and more beautiful than the one before. Anyone who owns a Stradivarius violin owns a treasure, a masterpiece of art.

We may not be able to sing, play, whittle or make a violin, but if we really want to, we will find a way to let the music out of our hearts and to praise God with it.

# A LEADER'S IMPACT
*Anonymous*

In September of 1862, the Civil War tilted decisively in favor of the South. The morale of the Northern army dipped to its lowest point of the war. Large numbers of Union troops were in full retreat in Virginia. Northern leaders began to fear the worst. They saw no way to reverse the situation and turn the beaten, exhausted troops into a useful army again.

There was only one general with the ability to work such a miracle. That was General George McClellan. He had trained the men for combat and they admired him. But neither the War Department nor the rest of the Cabinet members saw the connection. Only President Abraham Lincoln recognized Gen. McClellan's leadership skills.

Fortunately, Lincoln ignored the protests of his advisors and reinstated McClellan back in command. He told the general to go down to Virginia and give those soldiers something no other man on earth could give them: enthusiasm, strength and hope. McClellan accepted the command. He mounted his great black horse and cantered down the dusty Virginia roads.

What happened next is hard to describe. Northern leaders couldn't explain it. Union soldiers couldn't explain it either. Even McClellan couldn't quite explain what happened. Gen. McClellan met the retreating Union columns, waved his cap in the air and shouted words of encouragement. When the worn out men saw their beloved teacher and leader, they began to take heart once again. They were moved with an unshakable feeling that now things could be different, that finally things could be all right again.

Bruce Catton, the great Civil War historian, describes this excitement that grew when word spread that McClellan was back in command. "Down mile after mile of Virginia roads the stumbling columns came alive. Men threw their caps and knapsacks into the air, and yelled until they could yell no more...because they saw this dapper little rider outlined against the purple starlight.

"And this, in a way, was the turning point of the war....No one could ever quite explain how it happened. But whatever it was, it gave President Lincoln and the North what was needed. And history was forever changed because of it."

The story of Gen. McClellan illustrates dramatically the impact a leader can have on the human spirit.

## THE LITTLE GUY WITH A BIG DREAM
*Donna Menis*

Mike Iuzzolino, better known as Izz, is a young man who lives to play basketball. At just 13 years old he made the decision to quit playing other sports and to concentrate all his energies on playing basketball.

At an early age Mike developed the discipline to practice, practice, practice. It was not uncommon to see him dribbling a basketball while carrying his books. This self-discipline eventually evolved into a daily workout ritual. Every morning before school he lifted weights and shot 100 free throws. Every afternoon before practice he tossed 100 jump shots. During the summer, he often played long into the evening on a court in the alley next to his house, using the streetlight to see the hoop.

He became a standout point guard at Altoona High School in Pennsylvania, and won all-state honors his senior year.

Despite his outstanding shooting ability, Mike didn't attract the attention of very many major college basketball programs. You see, Izz was only five-feet, ten-inches tall, trying to make it in a "big" man's game. Penn State did offer him a scholarship, however, and Mike grabbed at the chance to continue playing ball at the college level.

During his freshman and sophomore years at Penn State, Mike spent most of his time on the bench, and averaged only 2.8 points a game. He was frustrated, but not discouraged. He continued his personal practice rituals. When he wasn't practicing, he was studying. He became an honor student.

At the end of his sophomore year, Mike decided to leave Penn State. He wanted to play the game he loved; however, it looked like he wouldn't be getting much "PT" (play time) at Penn State.

He transferred to Saint Francis College, a small liberal arts college in Loretto, PA, only 30 minutes from his home. He could not play basketball his first year at Saint Francis because of NCAA transfer regulations, but he did continue his personal daily practice. Once again Mike Iuzzolino was on the bench watching others play the game he loved.

When his chance did come the next year, Mike made the most of it. He averaged 21 points per game his junior season and 24 his senior year. Izz finished among the nation's leaders in three major scoring categories, making him the best all-around shooter in the country. Mike was named "Player of the Year" in the Northeast Conference and "Most Valuable Player" of the conference tournament.

Mike won in the classroom as well. He was twice named a first team Academic All-American. Mike also was recognized as the Mercedes-Benz Scholar-Athlete of the Year and "Champions" Scholar-Athlete, earning him scholarships for graduate school.

Mike's lifelong dream of making it to the NCAA tournament became a reality on a March evening in Loretto, when Saint Francis' Red Flash team defeated a heavily favored Fordham squad to win the first ever NCAA play-in game and gain a berth as one of 64 teams in the annual "March Madness" tournament.

For most people, what Mike Iuzzolino had overcome—lack of height, lack of playing time, lack of national media attention—was a lifetime's worth of adversity. Now Izz could enjoy what he had persevered so hard to accomplish.

However, Mike had one more dream—the most fantastic one of all. He wanted to play in the National Basketball Association. Never mind that only two percent of all college players ever make it to the NBA. Never mind that, as one sportscaster put it, "Five-foot, ten-inch guys aren't supposed to be drafted by the NBA."

Don't tell that to Mike. Taking advantage of the opportunity to demonstrate his deadly three-point shooting accuracy during pre-draft camps, Izz won over all doubters and showed that he could play with the big guys. On June 26, 1991, in the NBA draft, Mike Iuzzolino was the 35th pick, a second round choice of the Dallas Mavericks.

The axiom still holds...most little guys don't stand a chance of making it to the NBA. But little guys with big dreams who possess courage and determination do make it.

## "NOTHING WILL GROW THERE!"
### Brian Cavanaugh, T.O.R.

Each summer as I bite into a juicy, homegrown tomato, I think of a humorous event concerning a time, as a seminary student, when three of us sought permission to plant a garden. Our house of studies was located in the downtown area of a large metropolitan city. There wasn't much of a backyard. Actually, it was a stone-covered dirt parking lot with no extra space. However, we carefully planned our garden, taking into account the area that received optimal sunshine.

The three of us approached the superior with our plan for a small area to plant some squash, tomatoes and cucumbers. The only real cost involved was to rent a rake, a pick-ax and a hoe. However, getting the superior's permission would still be difficult. None of us who were involved with this garden project will ever forget his response to our request. With a slightly bored tilting of his head, he glanced at us and abjectly replied, "You're wasting your time. Nothing will ever grow there! But, go ahead if you still want to."

We had received permission from on high! So what if it wasn't enthusiastic. We rented tools; raked four inches of stones into neat walls outlining the garden; hoisted the pick-ax and struck what must have been a former refuse area. A gardener's dream—dark, composted, fertile soil just sitting there waiting to be discovered. We looked at each other with broad grins and repeated in unison, "Ah, nothing will grow there."

As you might have surmised by now, things did grow there, in our garden. In fact, twice we re-staked the tomatoes, topping them off, finally, when they were seven feet tall. They seemed more like tomato trees than plants.

Whenever a group of us from those seminarian days get together, the story of our little garden is retold. "Nothing will ever grow there!"

Isn't it amazing how much can be learned from planting a garden—about life, about people? How often have you said about another person, whether elderly, middle aged, a teenager, or a child, that nothing will ever grow there? Perhaps all that is needed is for someone to help that person rake away some of the stones that are covering up the rich, fertile soil-of-life, just waiting to be discovered.

# WORK WITH FLAWS
*Anonymous*

There is a story about two men, both Italian sculptors and contemporaries, named Donatello and Michelangelo. One day Donatello received delivery of a huge block of marble. After examining it carefully, Donatello rejected the marble because it was too flawed and cracked for him to use.

Now this was long before forklifts and hydraulic lifts, so the workmen moved the heavy load by using a series of log rollers. Rather than struggle back to the quarry, the quick-thinking haulers decided to deliver it down the street to Michelangelo. After all, he was known to be a little absent-minded. He might not realize that he had not ordered a three-ton block of marble.

When Michelangelo inspected the marble, he saw the same cracks and flaws, as did Donatello. But he also saw the block as a challenge to his artistic skills. It became a personal challenge he could not pass up. So Michelangelo accepted the block of marble that Donatello had already rejected as too flawed and too cracked to be of any use.

Michelangelo proceeded to carve from that seemingly useless block of marble what is considered to be one of the world's greatest art treasures—the statue "David."

## WE'VE LOST SIGHT OF CHRISTMAS
*Brian Cavanaugh, T.O.R.*

During the frenzied pace of the Christmas season, we tend to lose sight of the message and promise that Christmas heralds. So often we're caught up in getting ready for this's and last minute that's. We rush here. We push there, and practically run over people seeking that special gift which we really cannot afford.

Could all this hurrying and scurrying be Satan's vengeance against God, or his revenge against the Incarnation—the birth of the Son of God? Satan blinds us all with the glitter and gloss, sounds of bells tingling and cash registers jingling. We've lost sight of the meaning of Christmas—the message of peace among all men and women, the promise of joy to everyone of good will.

Christmas' true splendor is found more often in simplicity—simplicity rooted in awareness and listening. For as we listen more to the world around us, we become increasingly aware of the troubles and pain, the anger and strain that men and women suffer. It is the message and promise of Christmas which can bring hope to the little, the lost and the least; to the bruised, the battered and the broken.

47

One of the greatest gifts we can bring to the world, bring to each man, woman or child we meet this Christmas season, is to "practice random kindness and senseless acts of beauty." I'm reminded of the *B.C.* comic strip from several years ago in which cartoonist Johnny Hart has the character Wiley searching for answers to one of life's great questions. It is a question so simple and yet so timely. In the first panel Wiley asks, "Whatever happened to kindness?" He then proceeds to write the following verse:

"Why do people go to the trouble
　　to give other people some trouble?
Why do they burst someone's bubble,
　　when they know it comes back to them double?
Why do we go to the effort to hurt
　　someone we actually love?
Why can't we say something sweet 'stead of curt?
　　A push only leads to a shove.
Why can't we treat other folks with respect?
　　With a smile or a kind word or two?
Treat them with honor, the way you'd expect
　　they should act when they're dealing with you.
Why can't we overlook others' mistakes?

We've all surely been there before.
Love and forgiveness is all that it takes,
to boot Satan's butt out the door."

This Christmas season, give a gift that will last, a gift that will endure long after you are gone. "Practice random kindness and senseless acts of beauty." Go ahead, try it! It will shock you only a bit. I'm sure it will astound others, too, and I am certain it will startle the world around you. Go ahead, practice kindness anyway. The world could use a jolt such as this.

## STILL ROPE, STILL HOPE
### *Anonymous*

A story is told about an oilman who started to drill a new well on his land. In oil field jargon, the drilling pipe is called a "rope."

After drilling a deep hole, there was no oil to be found. The owner decided that it was a dead hole, and told the crew boss to cap the well. He would write it off as a complete loss.

Meanwhile, the foreman called to the driller and asked how much "rope" was left on the rig. "About six to eight feet," replied the driller.

"Then keep on drilling deeper," shouted the foreman.

After drilling only two feet more, the well struck oil, and was one of the most productive wells in the entire oil field.

We can learn a lot about life from the drilling of an oil well; while there is still rope, there is still room for hope.

## BE A LAMPLIGHTER
### Brian Cavanaugh, T.O.R.

Several parents were sitting on a neighbor's porch discussing their children. They were talking about the negative environment in which the kids had to grow up—an environment filled with drugs, violence, and a pervading feeling of hopelessness. How could they, the parents, bring any light into their children's world since it seems so dark and hopeless? Could they be enough of a positive influence in their children's lives that the children would not just survive, but possibly work to change the world around them? The discussion went on for some time.

One of the parents, a science teacher, remarked, "I think we can make a difference in our children's lives if we become lamplighters."

"Lamplighters? What do you mean?" the others asked.

She explained. "Around the turn of the century a lamplighter went around the streets lighting the streetlamps. He carried a long pole that had a small candle on top with which he would reach up to light the kerosene-fed lamps. But from a distance you could not see a lamplighter very well. The light from

51

one small candle was not very bright in the surrounding darkness of night.

"However," she continued, "you could follow the progress of the lamplighter as he went along a street. The presence of his candle was barely visible until it joined with the flame of the streetlamp being newly lit. A radiant glow erased a portion of the night's darkness, and looking back down the street, you could see that the light from the glowing streetlamps made the entire street bright as day. The darkness was held at bay."

Almost as a chorus the parents exclaimed, "That's it! We'll be lamplighters for our children. We'll be their role models. We'll share from our own flame in order to light each child's individual lamp of wisdom, and by our love provide the fuel necessary to nourish and sustain its flame. Then we will have helped them become bright enough themselves so that they can conquer the darkness and hopelessness of their world."

## A RIPPLE OF HOPE
### Robert F. Kennedy

When God made you, he threw away the mold.
There never has been or ever will be another person
like you. The late Robert F. Kennedy addressed the
young people of South Africa in 1966 with the following passage. The same passage was used by Ted
Kennedy in his eulogy at his brother Robert's funeral.

"Some believe there is nothing one man or one
woman can do against the enormous array of the
world's ills. Yet many of the world's great movements
of thought and action have flowed from the work of a
single person....

"These people moved the world, and so can we all.
Few will have the greatness to bend history itself, but
each person can work to change a small portion of
events, and in the total of all those acts will be written
the history of this generation.

"It is from numberless diverse acts of courage and
belief that human history is shaped. Each time a person stands up for an ideal, or acts to improve the lot of
others, or strikes out against injustice, he or she sends

forth a tiny ripple of hope. And crossing each other from a million different centers of energy and daring, those ripples build a current that can sweep down the mightiest walls of oppression and resistance."

# ANSWER TO PRAYER
*Anonymous*

Years ago an old lady down south had no money to buy food. But with complete trust in God, she got down on her knees and prayed aloud: "Dear Lord, please send me a side of bacon and a sack of cornmeal."

Over and over again the old lady repeated the same plea in a loud voice. Now, one of the town's most detestable characters, overhearing her supplication, decided to play a trick on her. Hurrying to the nearest store, he bought a side of bacon and a sack of cornmeal. Upon his return to the cabin, he dropped the food down the chimney. It landed right in front of the hungry woman as she knelt in prayer.

Jumping to her feet, she exclaimed jubilantly, "O Lord, you've answered my prayer!" Then she ran all around the neighborhood telling everyone the good news.

This was too much for the scoundrel. He ridiculed her before the whole town by telling how he had dropped the food down the chimney himself. The wise old woman quickly replied, "Well, the devil may have brought it, but it was the Lord who sent it!"

# GROWING OLDER
*Anonymous*

When the poet Henry Wadsworth Longfellow was well along in years, his hair was white but he was still a vigorous man. Someone asked him why this was so.

The poet pointed to an apple tree in bloom and said, "That tree is very old, but I never saw prettier blossoms on it than it now bears. That tree grows new wood each year. Like that apple tree, I try to grow a little new wood each year."

# YOUR EASTER
*Anonymous*

A college girl was on a plane flying from Pittsburgh to her home. As she stared out of the plane window down at the green countryside below, her heart was heavy and tears were in her eyes.

She was a student returning home for the Easter holidays. Her first year of college was nearly over and it was a disaster. She was convinced that life no longer held any real meaning for her. Her only ray of happiness lay in the fact that she would soon see the ocean, which she loved dearly.

As the plane touched down on the runway, the girl wondered what kind of Easter vacation was possible after having such a difficult time in college.

Her grandmother met her at the gate, and the two of them drove to her home in complete silence. As they pulled into the driveway the girl's only thought was getting to the ocean.

It was well after midnight when she arrived at the beach. What happened next is best described in her own words. She says, "I just sat there in the moonlight watching the waves roll up on the beach. Slowly my disastrous first year passed before my eyes, day by day, week by week, month by month. Then, suddenly, the whole experience fell into place. It was over and past. I could forget about it forever; but at the same time, I didn't want to forget it.

"The next thing I knew, the sun was rising in the east. As it did I sensed my feelings starting to peak, just as a wave starts to peak before it breaks. That morning I, too, arose!

"It was as though my mind, heart and body were drawing strength from the ocean. All my old goals, dreams and enthusiasm came rushing back stronger than ever. I rose with the sun, got into my car, and headed for home."

After her Easter vacation that girl returned to college, picked up the broken pieces of her year, and fitted them back together again. In the short span of an Easter vacation, that girl died and rose again. For the first time in her life she understood the practical meaning of Easter.

## NEW CREATURES IN CHRIST
*Anonymous*

Queen Victoria once paid a visit to a paper mill. Without knowing who this distinguished visitor was, the foreman showed her the workings of the mill. She went into the rag-sorting shop where employees picked out the rags from the refuse of the city. Upon inquiring what was done with this dirty mass of rags, she was told that it would eventually make the finest white writing paper. After her departure, the foreman found out who it was that had paid the visit.

Some time later, Her Majesty received a package of the most delicate, pure white stationery, bearing the Queen's likeness for a watermark. Enclosed was a note saying that the stationery had been made from the dirty rags she had recently inspected.

This story illustrates Christ's work in us, as well. He takes us, filthy as we are, and makes us into new creatures. After receiving Jesus, we are as spiritually different from what we were before, as pure white paper is from the filthy rags from which it is made.

# CONSIDER THE WALNUT
*Anonymous*

Consider the walnut! If you compare a walnut with some of the beautiful and exciting things that grow on our planet, it does not seem to be a marvelous act of creation. It is common looking, rough, not particularly attractive, and certainly not monetarily valuable.

Besides, it is small. Its growth is limited by the hard shell that surrounds it, the shell from which it never escapes on its own.

Of course, though, that's the wrong way to judge a walnut.

Break a walnut open and look inside. See how the walnut has grown to fill every nook and cranny available to it. It had no say in the size or shape of that shell, but, given those limitations, it achieved its full potential of growth.

How lucky we will be if, like the walnut, we blossom and bloom in every space of life that is given to us.

Take heart! If one nut can do it, so can you.

## POWER TO FLY
*Anonymous*

Ultimately we have the power to decide what we believe about ourselves. Don't allow people to impose limitations on what you can do or whom you can become. Take, for instance, the humble bumble bee.

Biologists have determined that, aerodynamically speaking, the bumble bee cannot fly. It has too large of a body mass to be supported by such puny wings. The bumble bee fortunately does not listen to such criticism.

Remember: People rise no higher than their expectation level. Expect little, receive little. Expect to fly and who knows where your next flower might be?

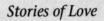

*Stories of Love*

# GRAINS OF CARING
## *Anonymous*

*T*wo brothers worked together on the family farm. One was married and had a large family. The other was single. At the day's end, the brothers shared everything equally, produce and profit.

Then one day the single brother said to himself, "It's not right that we should share equally the produce and the profit. I'm alone and my needs are simple." So each night he took a sack of grain from his bin and crept across the field between their houses, dumping it into his brother's bin.

Meanwhile, the married brother said to himself, "It's not right that we should share the produce and the profit equally. After all, I'm married and I have my wife and my children to look after me for years to come. My brother has no one, and no one to take care of his future." So each night he took a sack of grain and dumped it into his single brother's bin.

Both men were puzzled for years because their supply of grain never dwindled. Then one dark night the two brothers bumped into each other. Slowly it dawned on them what was happening. They dropped their sacks and embraced one another.

# GOD SEARCHES FOR US
## Anonymous

You may remember the story of Helen of Troy. According to legend this beautiful queen was captured and carried away and became a victim of amnesia. She became a prostitute in the streets. She didn't know her name or the fact that she came from royal blood. But back in her homeland, friends didn't give up hope for her return. An old friend believed she was alive and went to look for her. He never lost faith.

One day while wandering through the streets, he came to a waterfront and saw a wretched woman in tattered clothes with deep lines across her face. There was something about her that seemed familiar, so he walked up to her and said, "What is your name?" She gave a name that was meaningless to him. "May I see your hands?" he pursued. She held her hands out in front of her, and the young man gasped, "You are Helen! You are Helen! Do you remember?"

She looked up at him in astonishment. "Helen!" he yelled out. Then the fog seemed to clear. There was recognition in her face. The light came on! She discovered her lost self, put her arms around her old friend and wept. She discarded the tattered clothes and once more became the queen she was born to be.

God searches for you in the same way. He uses every method possible to look for you and try to convince you of your worth to him.

# GOD'S PATTERN IN OUR LIVES
*Anonymous*

A poor but honest jeweler was arrested for a crime he never committed. He was placed in a secure and well-protected prison in the center of the city. One day, after he had been imprisoned for months, his wife came to the main gate. She told the guards how her husband, the poor jeweler, was a devout and prayerful man. He would be lost without his simple prayer rug. Would they not permit him to have this single possession? The guards agreed that it would be harmless and gave him the prayer rug. Five times daily he would unroll his rug and pray.

Weeks passed, and one day the jeweler said to his jailers, "I'm bored sitting here day after day with nothing to do. I am a good jeweler and, if you will let me have some pieces of metal and some simple tools, I will make you exquisite pieces of jewelry. You can sell what I make in the bazaar and add to your low salaries as civil servants. I ask for so little—just something to fill the idle hours and keep my skill in practice."

The poorly paid jailers agreed that it would be a good arrangement. Each day they brought the jeweler some bits of silver and other metals, and a few simple tools. Each night they would remove the tools and metals and take home the jewelry that he had made for them.

Days grew into weeks, weeks into months. One bright morning when they came to the jeweler's cell, they found it empty! No sign was found of the prisoner or how he had escaped from this secure and well-protected prison.

Some time later, the real criminal was arrested for the crime of which the poor jeweler had been falsely accused. One day in the city's bazaar, one of the prison guards spotted the ex-prisoner, the jeweler. Quickly explaining that the real criminal was caught, he asked the jeweler how he had escaped. The jeweler proceeded to tell an amazing story.

The jeweler's wife had gone to the chief architect who had designed the prison. She obtained from him the blueprints to the cell door locks. She then designed a pattern and weaved it into a prayer rug. Five times each day he would pray, his head touching the rug. Slowly, he began to see that there was a design within a design, within yet another design, and it was the pattern for the lock of his cell door. From the bits of leftover metal and the simple tools, he fashioned a key and escaped!

# THE GIFT OF THE MAGI (adapted)
## O. Henry

A story is told about a young married couple whose names are Jim and Della. They are poor but very much in love with each other.

As Christmas approaches, Della wonders what to get Jim for Christmas. She would like to give him a watch chain for his gold watch, but she doesn't have enough money. Then she gets an idea. She has beautiful long hair. So Della decides to cut off her hair and sell it to buy the fancy chain for Jim's watch.

On Christmas Eve she returns home, and in her hand is a beautiful box containing a gold watch chain which she purchased by selling her hair. Suddenly Della begins to worry. She knows Jim admired her long hair, and she wonders if he will be disappointed that she cut it off and sold it.

Della climbs the final flight leading to their tiny apartment. She unlocks the door and is surprised to find Jim home and waiting for her. In his hand is a neatly wrapped box containing his gift he purchased for her.

When Della removes her scarf Jim sees Della's short hair, and tears well up in his eyes. But he says nothing. He chokes back the tears and gives Della the gift box.

When Della opens it, she can't believe her eyes. There in the box is a set of beautiful silver combs for her long hair.

And when Jim opens his gift, he, too, is astonished. There inside the box is a beautiful gold chain for his gold pocket watch. Only then does Della realize that Jim pawned his gold watch to buy her the silver hair combs.

Far more beautiful than the gifts is the love they symbolize.

# A MOTHER'S PARAPHRASE OF 1 CORINTHIANS 13
*Mrs. Mervin Seashore*

Though I speak with the language of educators and psychiatrists and have not love, I am as blaring brass or a crashing cymbal.

And if I have the gift of planning my child's future and understanding all the mysteries of the child's mind and have ample knowledge of teenagers, and though I have all faith in my children, so that I could remove their mountains of doubts and fears and have not love, I am nothing.

And though I bestow all my goods to feed and nourish them properly, and though I give my body to backbreaking housework and have not love, it profits me not.

Love is patient with the naughty child and is kind. Love does not envy when a child wants to move to grandma's house because "she is nice."

Love is not anxious to impress a teenager with one's superior knowledge.

Love has good manners in the home—does not act selfishly or with a martyr complex, is not easily provoked by normal childish actions.

Love does not remember the wrongs of yesterday and love thinks no evil—it gives the child the benefit of the doubt.

Love does not make light of sin in the child's life (or in her own, either), but rejoices when he or she comes to a knowledge of the truth.

Love does not fail. Whether there be comfortable surroundings, they shall fail; whether there be total communication between parents and children, it will cease; whether there be good education, it shall vanish.

When we were children, we spoke and acted and understood as children, but now that we have become parents, we must act maturely.

Now abides faith, hope, and love—these three are needed in the home. Faith in Jesus Christ, eternal hope for the future of the child, and God's love shed in our hearts, but the greatest of these is love.

## GOD WHO ENABLES
### Faye Sweeney

"It is God who enables you
to smile in spite of tears;
to carry on when you feel like giving in;
to pray when you're at a loss for words;
to love even though your heart has been broken
    time and time again;
to sit calmly when you feel like throwing up your
    hands in frustration;
to be understanding when nothing seems to
    make sense;
to listen when you'd really rather not hear;
to share your feelings with others, because sharing
    is necessary to ease the load.
Anything is possible,
because God makes it so."

# MEANING OF CHRISTMAS
*Anonymous*

Once upon a cold Christmas Eve, a man sat in reflective silence before the flames flickering in the fireplace, thinking about the meaning of Christmas. "There is no point to a God who became human," he mused. "Why would an all-powerful God want to share even one of his precious moments with the likes of us? And even if he did, why would God choose to be born in a stable? No way! The whole thing is absurd! I'm sure that if God really wanted to come down to earth, he would have chosen some other way."

Suddenly, the man was roused from his musings by a strange sound outside. He sprang to the window and leaned on the sash. Outside he saw a gaggle of snow geese frantically honking and wildly flapping their wings amid the deep snow and frigid cold. They seemed dazed and confused. Apparently, due to exhaustion, they had dropped out of a larger flock migrating to a warmer climate.

Moved to compassion, the man bundled up and went outside. He tried to "shoo" the shivering geese into the warm garage, but the more he "shooed," the more the geese panicked. "If they only realized that I'm trying to save them," he thought to himself. "How can I make them understand my concern for their well-being?"

Then a thought came to him: "If for just a minute, I could become one of them, if I could become a snow goose and communicate with them in their own language, then they would know what I'm trying to do."

In a flash of inspiration, he remembered it was Christmas Eve. A warm smile crossed his face. The Christmas story no longer seemed absurd. He visualized an ordinary-looking infant lying in a manger in a stable in Bethlehem. He understood the answer to his Christmas problem: God became one-like-us to tell us, in human terms that we can understand, that he loves us, that he loves us right now, and that he is concerned with our well-being.

# THE MOST VALUABLE TREASURE
## *Anonymous*

There is a city in Germany named Weinsberg. Overlooking the city, perched atop a high hill, stands an ancient fortress. The townspeople of Weinsberg are proud to tell about an interesting legend concerning the fortress.

According to the legend, in the 15th century, in the days of chivalry and honor, enemy troops laid siege to the fortress and sealed all the townsfolk inside. The enemy commander sent word up to the fortress announcing that he would allow the women and children to leave and go free before he launched a devastating attack.

After some negotiations, the enemy commander also agreed, on his word of honor, to let each woman take with her the most valuable, personal treasure she possessed, provided she could carry it out herself.

You can imagine the enemy commander's consternation and surprise when the women began marching out of the fortress...each one carrying her husband on her back.

## THE WEDDING RING
*Anonymous*

Some years ago divers located a 400-year-old sunken ship off the coast of Ireland. Among the treasures they found on the ship was a man's wedding ring. When it was cleaned up, the divers noticed that the ring had an inscription on it. Etched on the wide band were two hands holding a heart. Under the etching were these words: "I have nothing more to give you."

Of all the treasure found on that sunken ship, none moved the divers more than that ring and its beautiful inscription.

# LOVE FOR OTHERS: A HASIDIC STORY
## *Anonymous*

A wealthy Jewish merchant treats a poor old man with rudeness and disdain as they travel together on a train. When they arrive at their common destination, the merchant finds the station thronged with pious Jews waiting in ecstatic joy to greet the arrival of one of the holiest rabbis in Europe, and learns to his chagrin that the old man in his compartment is that saintly rabbi.

Embarrassed at his disgraceful behavior and distraught that he missed a golden opportunity to speak in privacy to a wise and holy man, the merchant pushes his way through the crowd to find the old man. When he reaches him, he begs the rabbi's forgiveness and requests his blessing. The old rabbi looks at him and replies, "I cannot forgive you. To receive forgiveness you must go out and beg it from every poor old person in the world."

# ON COMPASSION
*Anonymous*

Three old men, one of whom had a bad reputation, came one day to Abba Achilles. The first old man asked him, "Father, make me a fishing net." "I will not make you one," Abba replied.

Then the second said, "Of your charity make one, so that we have a souvenir of you in the monastery." But Abba Achilles said, "I do not have time."

Then the third one, who had the bad reputation, said, "Make me a fishing net, Father." Abba Achilles answered him at once, "For you, I will make one."

Then the two other old men asked him privately, "Why did you not want to do what we asked you, but you promised to do what he asked?"

Abba Achilles gave them this answer: "I told you I would not make one, and you were not disappointed, since you thought that I had no time. But if I had not made one for him, he would have said, 'The old man has heard about my sin, and that is why he does not want to make me anything,' and so our relationship would have broken down. But now I have cheered his soul, so that he will not be overcome with grief."

## THREE QUESTIONS
### *Anonymous*

The stage curtain opens. An actor walks onto the darkly lighted set and directs three questions out of the shadows toward the audience:

> 1. Is anyone there?
> 2. Is anyone listening?
> 3. Does anyone care?

# HEROES
## *Anonymous*

Babe Ruth had hit 714 home runs during his baseball career and was playing one of his last full major league games. It was the Braves vs. the Reds in Cincinnati. But the great Bambino was no longer as agile as he had been. He fumbled the ball and threw badly, and in one inning alone his errors were responsible for most of the five runs scored by Cincinnati.

As the Babe walked off the field and headed toward the dugout after the third out, a crescendo of yelling and booing reached his ears. Just then a boy jumped over the railing onto the playing field. With tears streaming down his face, he threw his arms around the legs of his hero.

Ruth didn't hesitate for a second. He picked up the boy, hugged him and set him down on his feet, patting his head gently. The noise from the stands came to an abrupt halt. Suddenly there was no more booing. In fact, a hush feel over the entire park. In those brief moments, the fans saw two heroes: Ruth, who, in spite of his dismal day on the field, could still care about a little boy; and the small lad, who cared about the feelings of another human being. Both had melted the hearts of the crowd.

# LOVING YOUR ENEMIES
*Anonymous*

Abraham Lincoln tried to love, and he left for all history a magnificent drama of reconciliation. When he was campaigning for the presidency, one of his arch-enemies was a man named Edwin McMasters Stanton. For some reason Stanton hated Lincoln. He used every ounce of his energy to degrade Lincoln in the eyes of the public. So deep-rooted was Stanton's hate for Lincoln that he uttered unkind words about his physical appearance, and sought to embarrass him at every point with the bitterest diatribes. But in spite of this, Lincoln was elected the sixteenth president of the United States of America.

Then came the period when Lincoln had to select his cabinet, which would consist of the persons who would be his most intimate associates in implementing his programs. He started choosing men here and there for the various positions.

The day finally came for Lincoln to select the all-important post of Secretary of War. Can you imagine whom Lincoln chose to fill this post? None other than the man named Stanton. There was an immediate uproar in the president's inner circle when the news began to spread. Advisor after advisor was heard saying, "Mr. President, you are making a mistake. Do you know this man Stanton? Are you familiar with all the ugly things he said about you? He is your enemy. He will seek to sabotage your programs. Have you thought this through, Mr. President?"

Mr. Lincoln's answer was terse and to the point: "Yes, I know Mr. Stanton. I am aware of all the terrible things he has said about me. But after looking over the nation, I find he is the best man for the job." So Stanton became Abraham Lincoln's Secretary of War and rendered an invaluable service to his nation and his president.

Not many years later Lincoln was assassinated. Many laudable things were said about him. But of all the great statements made about Abraham Lincoln, the words of Stanton remain among the greatest. Standing near the dead body of the man he once hated, Stanton referred to him as one of the greatest men who ever lived and said, "He now belongs to the ages."

If Lincoln had hated Stanton both men would have gone to their graves as bitter enemies. But through the power of love Lincoln transformed an enemy into a friend. This is the power of redemptive love.